# THE RIDICULOUSLY SIMPLE GUIDE TO APPLE WATCH SERIES 4

A PRACTICAL GUIDE TO GETTING STARTED WITH THE NEXT GENERATION OF APPLE WATCH AND WATCHOS 5

SCOTT LA COUNTE

Ridiculously Simple Press
ANAHEIM, CALIFORNIA

# Contents

# INTRODUCTION

The stage was set in September 2018. It was iPhone's big event. The day where journalist and Apple fans alike lusted over the latest and greatest iPhone. But a funny thing happened on the way to the announcement: Apple Watch Series 4 took everyone's breath away!

The Apple Watch has, of course, been around for three years and seen several updates. But 2018 was different: the watch was finally ready for the masses. This wasn't a watch for early adopters or fitness buffs--this was the watch your parents and grandparents would get behind.

In addition to all the great features Apple Watch has always had, series 4 is slimmer (yet with a screen that is somehow bigger), has optional cellular for making phone calls and streaming music without your phone, and drop detection (so if you fall and can't get up, the fire department is dispatched to your location). Everything about it was designed to motivate you to be more active.

As amazing as all the new features are, it's not quite as easy to use as an iPhone; the lack of buttons, the smaller screen, and general UI can make a frustrated initial experience. The point of this book is to help new Apple Watch users (and users updating to Watch OS 5 from an older device) get the most out their investment.

Are you ready to start enjoying your new Apple Watch? Then let's get started!

# [1]

# IS APPLE WATCH *REALLY* THE BEST SMARTWATCH OUT THERE?

This chapter will cover:
- Learn about other smartwatches
- Learn how Apple Watch is similar and different

In terms of smartwatches, there's nothing that comes close to what Apple has built. Its menus are fluid, it's sleek, and, like other Apple products, it just works. But let's take a moment and look at how the other watches stack up against the Apple Watch.

**Android Wear**

If you have an Android phone, then Android Wear is the official watch for you. Apple Watch will not be supported by Android. Most Android Wear watches are $200 to $300 dollars—though there are several cheaper options in the sub-$50 range...but they are cheaper for a reason—they don't work like you'd expect; they are more often than not cheap plastic toys that only sort of do what you want.

Unlike Apple Watch, Android is open source and many fashion designers have created their own smart watches. Kate Spade, Marc Jacobs, and Michael Kors are just a few designers that you'll find on Android.

Most Android watches have batteries that last a day...like the Apple Watch; and most, like the Apple Watch have sensors to track health and fitness. There are also plenty of apps to load onto your watch.

So why is Apple Watch better than Android Wear? Opinions obviously vary, but many feel that Apple Apps work smoother and everything is more fluid. Unlike Android, Apple screens their apps to make sure apps that don't really do anything don't get on the app store.

It should also be noted that WatchOS (Apple's operating system) is built for one watch; Android's Watch OS is customized for each watch, and some manufacturers don't put the effort into that customization that's needed to make the watch great. Some Android Watches are supported in some capacity on the iPhone, but not all.

**Pebble**

In terms of price, Pebble is the best watch for your money. The Pepple watch ceased to exist in 2016 (its intellectual property was sold to FitBit), but you can still find good deals on those 2016 models.

The Pebble watch is one of the few watches compatible with both Android and iPhone smartphones. The Pebble is not a bad watch, but it is a limited one. There is no touchscreen, graphics are subpar, and notifications are not as fluid as Apple Watch. It also won't win any fashion awards.

**Windows Band**

Windows also has a watch called the Windows Band. Calling it a watch is a bit of a stretch, however. While it does tell time, it's more of a high-end fitness band. At $199, most people will be left wondering why not just pay a little more for an Apple Watch or a little less for a Fitbit or Jawbone (both of which cost about $120).

**Fitbit**

And speaking of Fitbit, they've recently entered the smartwatch came with their $199 FitBit Versa. If you are looking for a watch purely for fitness and don't want to shell out more for the Apple Watch, then the Versa is your best bet.

# [2]

# SO MANY MODELS! WHAT'S RIGHT FOR ME?!

This chapter will cover:
- What's the difference between all the Series Watches
- Why pay more for Steel?
- What's the right model for me?

The Apple Watch comes in several different. Every watch--from the original Apple Watch to the Series 4 are compatible with any previous generation band. So if you have an original Apple Watch, you can still use that expensive band you may have picked up. You can also find third-party bands much cheaper on Amazon and other online retailers.

The Milanese Loop band from Apple, for example, retails for $149; the below example, looks the same but is less than $20! The quality is not the same, but if you just want something that looks nice, then this could be a good option. I'll cover bands in greater detail at the end of this book.

Each version of the watch comes in two sizes 38mm and 42mm on earlier models; 40mm and 44mm for Series 4; each version also comes in Aluminum and Stainless Steel--stainless steel is the most expensive

## Apple Watch Series 0 and 1
The Apple Watch is the watch that started everything; there was no "series" number--so when

you see Apple Watch Series 1, you aren't actually looking at the first edition of the watch.

This year is the first year that the original Apple Watch did not receive a WatchOS update (that means the people who paid upwards of $20,000 for a watch, now have a worthless piece of technology). It still works fine--it just doesn't have new features. You can't find it new anymore, but you probably can find a used one in decent shape for the low $100s.

The Apple Watch Series 1 is still supported (though it probably won't be next year) and you can get it certified refurbished on the Apple Store website starting at $169.

## Apple Watch Series 2

The Series 2 introduced water resistance and GPS to the watch. You might occasionally see it pop up on Apple Refurbished store, but it is no longer sold new.

## Apple Watch Series 3

Cellular was added to the Apple Watch Series 3. That means you can make calls from your watch even if your phone is nowhere nearby. It is currently the cheapest watch you can buy new at $279.

## Apple Watch Series 4

The Series 4 watch starts at $399. The biggest noticeable difference is cosmetic: it's bigger than previous generations, and yet it's also thinner and lighter. On the inside the processor is faster, the screen is brighter, and the battery lasts longer.

The Series 4 Apple Watch is considered the ultimate watch in fitness. It's also the watch you'll want to get your elderly parents and grandparents--it has drop detection and will automatically call for help if it detects you've fallen and don't respond.

Which watch is right for you? Unless you have an itching to spend 1k+ for a watch, then you are probably considering the steel model with Hermes band over the sports model. What's the difference? In terms of wear and tear, both watches will hold up pretty well; every watch—even the more expensive ones—have the same hardware. The steel model has a stronger display that is slightly more scratch-resistant.

Unlike the iPhone or iPad, you aren't paying more for more memory—you are paying for the finish—so it's really a question of taste. The steel watch is slick, smooth and shiny. If you can afford it and want something a little classier, than the steel watch is a good option.

If you are trying to decide between the series one and series two, it really comes down to how you will use it. If you're a swimmer and want to use your watch in the pool, then you definitely want the series 2 and up; the GPS on series 2 is also great for fitness and tracking where you go when your phone isn't next to you. Series 1 (and even the original Apple Watch) is still an excellent watch, however.

If you are trying to decide if you should buy the Series 3 or 4, my recommendation is spend a little more for the 4. It will be supported by WatchOS the longest. The largest display will also work better with newer apps being built for the watch.

Also, if you already have the watch and don't like the band that you like, you are able to return the band (even if it's opened) to any Apple store within 14 days for a band of equal value. (Note: this offer will not necessarily run forever, so check with your local store before going in for an exchange.)

## Apple Watch Series 0 vs. Series 4

The original Apple Watch is called Apple Watch; because Apple introduced series the next year, it's been affectionately referred to as Series 0. For the past several years, Apple has continued to support series 0 with updates. That changed with WatchOS 5.

That doesn't mean Series 0 is completely obsolete. You can pick it up used for less than $100 (a fraction of what they went for new), and they still work with phones--you'll just be running the old operating system. You'll also be stuck with a watch with not so great battery life.

If you want to see what a difference four generations makes, below is side by side shots of Series 0 and Series 4. The first image shows how Series 4 is a little more rounded at the corners. It's not as noticeable here, but the screen is also a little bigger--even though the watch is lighter. Series 4 is on the left, and Series 0 is on the right.

Next is a side-by-side shot of the two watches.

The rounded corners are a little more obvious in the next image.

A closer side-by-side shot reveals the thickness of the Series 0 as compared to the Series 4.

Finally, a shot of the back reveals how the sensors are different. Series 4 has one sensor as opposed to the 4 on the Series 0.

# [3]

# WILL THE APPLE WATCH DO THIS…

This chapter will cover:
- What the Apple Watch won't do
- What the Apple Watch will do without an iPhone nearby
- What the Apple Watch will do on Wi-Fi without a iPhone nearby

When you think about the watch, you might have certain expectations—perhaps it's watching Netflix from your wrist or FaceTime with your friends. So before continuing to how the watch works, let me cover really quickly the major things the watch cannot do (that some people think it can)—and can do.

## Things the Apple Watch won't do...

- Play videos. It can render very small clips, but don't plan on watching *Lord of Your Rings* on your wrist.
- Type messages (there is no onboard keyboard…just a microphone). You can scribble to type (we'll cover that later)
- Play games — while Apple Watch games do exist, the watch is a companion to the phone, and meant for viewing short messages…not playing games. So yes, you can play games, but this is not what you want to get to meet your gaming needs.
- Sync with non-Apple phones; the Apple Watch will not work with any phone but iPhone.
- Work with older phones; the Apple Watch is for iPhone 5 and up
- Work with traditional headphones; there's no audio input on the Apple Watch; it does work with Bluetooth headphones, but these are not included with the watch.
- Take a photo; you can view photos on the watch—you can even use it as an external viewfinder to take a photo on your iPhone—but the watch has no built-in camera.

## Apple Watch Without An iPhone Nearby

To be entirely clear, you must own an iPhone to use the Apple Watch. The watch is not compatible with Android or any other smartphone. But you don't have to take your iPhone everywhere to use the watch. And if you have cellular on the watch, there's more you can do here without your phone nearby. Here are some of the things you can do if you don't have your phone nearby:

- Set the time.
- Play music (you can put up to 2 GB of songs on your watch...to put it another way, that's about 500 songs).
- Track your run / exercise — it will keep a record of things like calories burned, heart rate, and distance / pace, and then sync it to your phone when you have it nearby again.
- Track your standing time and steps.
- See your photos—75 MB is reserved for photos.
- Read, delete and flag email that has come in.
- Use the alarm, stopwatch, and timer.
- Use Passbook to show tickets (like an airplane or concert ticket).
- Use ApplePay to buy things.

**Wi-Fi Without iPhone**

And here's what you can do if you don't have your phone, but you do have Wi-Fi:

- Send and receive text message, and use digital touch messages (i.e. drawing and tapping patterns to send as a message).
- Use Siri.

## This and That

A few other things you might need to know about the watch...

- It takes about two hours to fully charge your Apple Watch.
- It takes your iPhone's battery...kind of; because the watch talks to your phone, your phone's battery will be used. It's not significant, but it's enough that you might notice 30 minutes to an hour of usage gone by the end of the day that used to be there.
- There's a feature on the device called "Taptic Engine"--fancy sound, right? But what is it? The taptic engine lets you receive feedback on your wrist that feels like someone is tapping you.
- You can use it as a phone...sort of. Yes, it sounds very Dick Tracy-like to get phone calls on your wrist, but don't get too excited—it's a little awkward to use; to get the most out of it, you really need to put it up or near your mouth. And the audio that comes out of the speakers is subpar at best.
- It tells time! Well yes—you probably knew that. But it also tells time very precisely (within 50 milliseconds), which makes it one of the most accurate watches ever made.

# [4]

# OKAY, SO HOW DO I SET THIS THING UP?

This chapter will cover:
- Unboxing
- Setting up the Apple Watch for the first time
- Restoring from a previous generation Apple Watch

This chapter is all about taking it out of the box and setting it up for the first time. You might be perfectly comfortable doing this without reading how. If that's the case, then skip ahead to the next chapter--you won't miss anything here.

The process is pretty simple, but if you want an explanation of what it's actually doing in each step--like why it asked about privacy--then read on.

*NOTE TO USERS UPDATING: If you are updating your iPhone and Watch from a previous OS, there's a chance you will have to reformat your watch to get it to sync. If that happens, then from your watch you need to go to Settings / General / Reset; next tap Erase All Content and Settings.*

## Unboxing

And now the moment you've been waiting for--the unboxing! Or, as the girl at Target explained to me, the "You paid $399 for that little box?!"

Many readers already have the device and could care less about unboxing photos; some readers are still deciding and are curious about what's in that narrow rectangular box. For those readers, feast your eyes on the below.

There are actually two boxes in that box; one contains the watch, the charger, and the charger cord.

The other contains the watch band and the instructions for how to install the watch band.

## Setting Things Up

Once you have the watch out of the box, push the side button to turn it on. You get the following screen:

Because the Apple Watch has no keyboards, setup is a bit unusual compared to other Apple products. Setup for the watch actually begins not with the watch, but with the iPhone.

If you aren't running iPhone iOS 12 and up, then the first thing you need to do is update your phone. You also need at least an iPhone 5—anything less will not be compatible. To see if your phone needs to be updated, go to Settings on the iPhone, then General, and finally Software Update—it will tell you if your phone is up-to-date.

If you are up-to-date on everything, then go to the Watch app, and tap "Start Pairing". This gives you the below setup screen.

Place your watch (make sure it's turned on) within that square box (you'll notice your watch has a moving image on it's screen now. In just a few seconds, it will say your watch is paired.

From here you can either Restore from a backup or Set Up as a new watch. If you've never owned an Apple Watch (or you want to start fresh), then select the second choice. If you've owned previous generations, then select the first (this will put all your preferences from your old watch on your new watch). Assuming you are setting it up as a new watch, the next screen will ask if you are wearing the watch on your Left or Right wrist. Based on your answer, the orientation of the watch will change (you can change this later)

Next you'll need to agree to terms. Feel free to read it thoroughly through--then give it to your lawyer to ask what they think...or just hit Agree like everyone else. After you agree to the terms you'll get a message telling you some apps will use things like your location. That sounds scary, but what it basically means is if you want to use a map to get directions, then it has to know where you are first. Your only option here is to hit ok.

After you agree to share your location with apps, you need to add a passcode. This works much like your phone (before you phone had fingerprint to unlock or Face ID). You don't have to add a passcode. Adding it protects your watch from someone stealing it and then using it.

Is Apple breaking your heart with this setup? The next screen will help detect it! It tells you all about the new heart monitor feature. Read it and then hit continue.

Next is SOS. This feature will text your contacts to tell them if you are in trouble. It's sort of like Apple's version of "I've fallen and I can't get up." Read it and hit continue to proceed.

You may not have known it, but a lot of your favorite apps already have Watch apps. You can add everything that you already own, or pick and choose them later. Personally, I would be careful of selecting all of them. This is the easiest option, but you'll probably find a lot of your favorite phone apps are sort of pointless on your wrist.

You're just about done. Your phone and watch are now syncing with all the settings you just selected. If you decided to install all apps, it will take a few minutes to finish. Along the way you'll probably also get a message about your phone and watch now sharing text message--that just means if someone text you, you'll get it on your wrist to.

A message will now appear on both your phone and watch saying it's done. You can now use your watch!

# [5]

# ENOUGH WITH THE SETUP! SHOWING ME HOW TO USE THIS THING!

This chapter will cover:
- Adjusting settings
- What status icons represent
- Force Touch
- Gestures and shortcuts
- Arranging icons
- Handoff between Apple Watch and iPhone

Setup is pretty self-explanatory, right? What you *really* are waiting for is how to use this thing! So let's get started!

## Power on, Wake, and Unlock

To turn your watch on, press and hold the side button until the Apple logo appears; to turn it off press and hold the side button until a slider appears telling you to drag it to the right to power off.

Taking your phone off standby is the most seamless thing you'll do—just lift your wrist! How's that for easy? Turning standby back on is just as simple—put your wrist down.

If you lift your wrist and standby doesn't turn off, then it's possible that you changed a setting. Open the Setting button on the home screen of your watch (it looks just like the one on your phone except it's round, and then go to General and Orientation—make sure Orientation is set to the wrist that you wear—if you are wearing it on your right hand and Orientation is set to left hand, for example, then change it. The other thing that might have happened is your battery has drained.

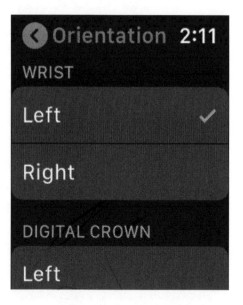

When you lift your wrist, the watch will either show your watch face (i.e. time) or the last app opened. By default it shows the watch face, but if you want it to go to your last activity, then go to Settings, then General, and finally Wake Screen—once you tap this, pick Resume Previous Activity.

You also have the ability to unlock the watch with your phone using a Passcode. This is a great feature if you take your watch off a lock. It doesn't mean you need to put in a passcode every time you look at the time—it only needs it when the watch is off your wrist or being worn too loosely. The Passcode can be the same as the phone, but it's recommended that the code is different. To activate Passcode, go to Settings from your watch's home screen, and then scroll down until you see Passcode, then tap it. Tap turn on Unlock with iPhone. If you ever want to change it, just follow the same steps, but pick Change Passcode.

If you ever forget your passcode, then unpair it from the iPhone and erase all the settings.

## Adjusting Text Size, Brightness, Sounds, and Haptics

I hope you love settings, because that's where we'll stay for this section!

The Apple Watch is probably smaller than you're used to when reading messages, emails, news, etc.; if it's too small then you can make text larger by going to Brightness and Text Size, tap Text Size and then use the Digital Crown knob to increase or decrease it. You can also check or un-check making the text boldface (Note: Before bold-face is in place the watch will need to be reset.).

From this same menu, you can adjust how bright the watch is.

If you don't like the default sounds on your watch, then go to Sounds & Haptics from the Settings menu. Use your Digital Crown knob to adjust how loud it gets. You can also mute sounds by switching to silent mode (Note: muting does not turn off sound on alarms).

If you school just a little more to the bottom, one fun option is the Tap to Speak Time for the Mickey Mouse watch display (only for this display). When this is on, anytime you tap the Mickey Mouse display, Mickey's voice will tell you the time. I'll cover how to change displays later in this book.

For some notifications, you will get a tap on your wrist, which you may love or hate. If you hate it, then go back to the previous menu. Next, go to the Haptic section and you can toggle it on or off-- and also make it more prominent.

## Charge the Apple Watch

Charging your watch is very simple; it might be a little strange at first, because the charger is magnetic and doesn't plug into the watch—rather it snaps into the back. Make sure you use the charger case that came with your device—using any other might overcharge the device, which will drain the battery quickly.

It takes about two hours to fully charge the watch.

If you want to know how much time is needed for a full charge, swipe up from the watch face, which brings up Glances, and then swipe to the Battery glance.

When the watch has less than 10% power left, it will automatically go into a Power Reserve mode—in this mode, the watch will show the time, but other apps won't be available. You can also manually turn Power Reserve on by pressing the side button for three seconds until the Power menu comes up, then swiping Power Reserve.

You can see how much time you have left in your battery reserve at any time by swiping up from the watch face to bring up Glances, then swiping to Power Reserve. You can also use the Apple Watch app on your iPhone to see the last time you charged it.

*NOTE: Anytime I mention glances in this book, that just means swipe up from you devices—jthere are a lot of Glances I'll be covering.*

### Settings on the iPhone

Now that we covered all the settings, then here's a hint you'll probably be annoyed I didn't tell you about earlier: you can do all of this on your phone!

You don't always have your phone on you, so you should know where they are on both the watch and the phone. Most people will find it easier to control settings on a larger device, however.

To adjust the settings, go to your Watch app on the phone, and then scroll down to the setting you want. Anything you change here will sync to your watch automatically. There's nothing else to do!

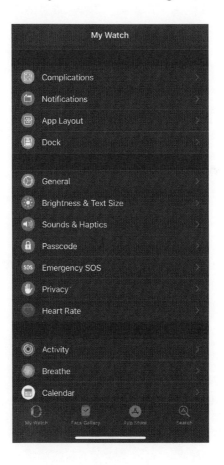

## Status Icons

Notifications on the Apple Watch come in many forms; one way is through status icons; these icons let you quickly glance down at your wrist and know there's a new email or your watch needs to be charged. Some are less obvious that others. The status icons and what they mean are listed below:

You have an unread notification such as an email.

The Apple Watch is charging.

Your battery is low.

The Apple Watch is locked and needs a passcode to use.

Your watch is in "Do Not Disturb" mode and will not make any sounds or light up until enabled again; alarms, however, will still work.

The Apple Watch is in Airplane mode and only non-wireless features work—Bluetooth and Wi-Fi are not turned on.

Your watch is in "Theater Mode" and stays silent and the screen stays dark unells you tap on the screen or press one of the buttons.

Your watch is connected to a wi-fi network instead of your phone.

This is something you'll only see on a Apple Watch with a cellular connection. It indicates you are connected to cellular; the bars indicate how strong the connection is. Four is the highest.

Again, this is only something you'll see on an Apple Watch with a cellular connection, and it means you have lost your cellular connection.

If you are swimming or doing something with lots of water, this indicates that water lock is on, and the watch will not respond to taps.

Swipe up to your glances and you'll see this icon; it represents your audio connection; tapping on this will let you switch audio from your watch to another device. So, for instance, if you are listening to music and want it to play on a wireless headset.

Location service is on. What does this mean? It means there's an app (such as Maps) that's using your location in the background.

Your watch is no longer paired with your phone.

There's wireless activity happening or some other kind of active event—an app loading for example.

If you are using the Workout app, then you'll see this status icon appear. Tap it to switch back to the app.

I'll cover the Walkie-Talkie feature later; for now, just understand that this icon represents that feature.

You'll see this icon when audio is playing.

## Gestures and Shortcuts

With such a limited space, Apple really made use of something called Gestures. Gestures is essentially your watch doing different things based on how you touch or swipe the watch. If you have an iPhone or Mac with Force Touch, you'll be somewhat familiar with this. If not, don't worry--it's easy to understand.

This section will give you a quick overview of the gestures and shortcuts that let you do what you need to do quickly.

### The Big Three

There are three actions that you'll use more than others.

### #1

The one shortcut you will use the most is the Digital Crown; pressing it will always get you back to the home screen. It's like the square button on your iPhone (if you have an iPhone that still has a home screen button).

### #2

Swiping down from the top edge of your watch face will get you notifications. If you missed a text or email or any other alert, then swipe down and you can see what it was. You probably know this gesture is exactly the same as your iPhone--Apple, whenever possible--tried to keep gestures the same or similar.

If you swipe left over a notification, you'll get two more options: clear and more options.

Clear does exactly what it sounds like--it clears! More options let's you change how a notification is delivered.

Notifications can start adding up really quick. Maybe you are the type who loves to go through each one and clear them individually; I find it time-consuming, and would rather clear them at once. That's easy! Just firm press on any notification (that means you touch it firmly and hold until a message pops up). When the Clear All message comes up, tap it. This won't delete the message--only the no-tification.

#3

Swipe up from the bottom edge of your watch face to see glances. Glances is a little like the Control Center on your iPhone--on older iPhones it's the same gesture to get there (swiping up); newer iPhones access this by swiping down at the upper right corner.

Glances are nothing more than shortcuts and toggles. All those Status Icons I just mentioned? A lot of them are turned on here.

So when you want Swim mode or Airplane mode turn on, for example, just go into glances and push the button. Push it again to turn it off. Some of the icons (like the battery percent icon) will open up more options.

One Status Icon not covered previously was the flashlight, which is one of the glance options. On your iPhone, the flashlight is pretty useful (and bright); on the watch? Not so much. On the watch, the display turns on, so you have "some" light, but it's not the same brightness of using your camera's flash like on the phone. Swiping will bring up the different kinds of flashlights (white, flashing white, and red). To turn it off, swipe down.

At the bottom of glances, there's an edit button. If you tap that, you'll be able to drag and drop icons around (you can't delete them); this way you can organize the icons in order of the ones you use the most.

## Force Touch

Force Touch measures not just what you are touching, but how hard you are touching it. On your watch/clock screen, pressing a little harder on the screen will let you change the watch face. In apps, Force Touch is used a bit like right clicking on a computer--it brings up options.

## Zooming

You may be used to pinching and zooming on your iPhone and iPad; be prepared to be disappointed...on a smaller screen this method just doesn't work. In its place is the digital crown, which can be used to zoom in and out by turning the knob. You can use it to magnify things like photos and maps.

## Turning off the Screen

There's no physical button to turn off the Apple Watch. To turn the screen off you can either put your hand down, or cover the watch with your hand. You can also silence alarms by covering your hand over the screen.

## Launching Siri

There are two quick ways to launch Siri: one, press and hold the Digital Crown; two, lift up your wrist and speak--no buttons are required. Previously, you'd have to say "Hey Siri"; that's no longer needed. The watch can detect you are lifting your wrist to speak and hears what you say.

## Locate your iPhone

If you can't find your iPhone, you can quickly ping it with your watch to see if it's nearby. Go to your watch face, swipe up to bring up Glances, then tap the phone icon.

This will make your phone start beeping (Note: for this to work you must enable Find My iPhone from iCloud).

## Airplane Mode

Most airlines will let you leave your watch turned on while you're flying, but they will want it in airplane mode (which turns off settings that might interfere with the plane).

To put the watch in Airplane Mode, go to your watch face, swipe up from the bottom to bring up Glances, and go to the Settings glance, then tap the button that looks like an airplane. Repeat the step to turn the mode off.

If you'd like the watch to go in Airplane Mode whenever your phone does, then go to the Apple Watch app, tap My Watch, then tap Airplane Mode and turn on Mirror iPhone. Repeat the step to disable.

## Side Button

To toggle between your most recently used apps, press the side button on from the watch face. This brings up all the apps like a rolodex.

Use the digital crown to scroll through them; tap once to open an app; swipe right to crash the app.

## Last App

Need to go back to the last app used quickly? Double click the digital crown.

## Apple Pay

To use Apple Pay, double tap the side button; it will come up with your credit card and tell you to put it near the reader (your phone does not need to be nearby); once it is by the reader you enter your passcode. Worried about someone taking your phone and using your credit card? It won't work when it's taken off your wrist.

When you get to a reader that supports Apple Pay, simply double tap the side button. If you want to use a different credit card, swipe to the left. When you find the card you want, turn it to face the reader. When the transactions goes through, you'll hear a beep and you'll feel a tap—this alerts you to the fact that the transaction is complete.

Before you can use Apple Pay, however, you need to set it up. This is done on the iPhone. From your iPhone, tap the Apple Watch app, and then scroll to "Add Credit or Debit Card," and then tap it. You can either use a card on file with iTunes or add a new card. In either case you'll have to add your security number (or the full number if you are adding a new card); depending on the card, you may need to verify with another step, which is usually a text message with a code from your bank.

When you get the code, just tap Verify and enter it. You're all set to use your watch to buy things!

### Handoff between the Apple Watch and iPhone

Handoff lets you toggle between your watch and your phone without losing your place. If you are reading an email on your watch, and want to reply on your phone, then go to your phone; handoff used to appear on the lock screen of your phone-- it's a little less obvious now. You now access handoff from your app switcher screen on the iPhone (see below)

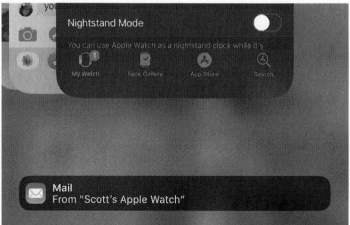

On a Macbook, handoff is in the doc.

You can turn Handoff on and off by opening the Apple Watch app on your iPhone, going to My Watch, then tapping on General and Enable Handoff.

## Arranging Icons

Arranging icons on the watch isn't that much different from arranging them on your iPhone or iPad. To start, go to your home screen, then touch and hold an app icon; you can now drag it to a new location.

To install a new app, open the Apple Watch app from your iPhone (Note: you have to use your iPhone to install apps), and then tap the App Store to find apps for the Apple Watch. Once you download them from your phone, you'll see a message on your watch asking if you want to install them. Just tap yes and you are done. When you are on the normal app store, you'll see a little round icon and "Offers Apple Watch App" if it's an app with a companion app for the watch.

The watch doesn't have as much room as your phone, so you might run out of space. To view how much storage is being used by an app, go to the Apple Watch app on the iPhone, then tap on My Watch, then go to General and Usage. Finally, view the storage being used by each app.

If you would like to remove an app, go to the home screen on the watch, then tap and hold the app you want to remove; when an X appears over the app, tap it. It will remain installed on your iPhone unless you remove it from there as well. Apps that were installed by Apple (such as the Settings button) cannot be removed.

If you find the screen a bit to small for rearranging icons, then you can also do it right from your iPhone; just open the Apple Watch app, tap the My Watch tab, and tap Layout. You rearrange the icons just as you would on your watch.

## SOS

SOS allows your Watch to call local emergency services to tell them your location; this is obviously something you only use in an emergency--it's not something try out just to see how it works! To enable it, hold the side button for 3 seconds, and then swipe SOS.

## Breathe

Breathe is a new app on the WatchOS 3 home screen. It's a free relaxation app designed to help calm your body after a workout or stressful day at work.

# [6]

# LET'S MAKE FACES...APPLE WATCH FACES, THAT IS!

This chapter will cover:
- What is a Apple Watch face
- How to change the Apple Watch face
- How to customize different Apple Watch faces

The Apple Watch has dozens of different faces to pick from—from traditional to modern to even a cute Mickey Mouse (and Minnie Mouse, of course). To change the watch's face, place your finger firmly over the current face for three seconds. The face will zoom back and you can swipe back and forth across your watch's screen to see different faces. Some watches you can customize; when that's possible you'll see a button that says Customize.

When you find the face that you want, tap it. Before tapping, however, you can also customize it by tapping the Customize button

You'll see dots at the top of the screen to indicate how much you can change. On the first screen, scroll with the knob to see what changes (it might, for instance, change the number of numbers on the watch). When you are done, swipe across the screen to get to the next customizable screen: colors. Using the knob, you can scroll through all of the colors. Swipe again, and you'll be at a screen that lets you add the current weather, calendar, etc. You'll tap on the screen to change any of these features, but first you have to swipe the Off to On.

After you have customized the face to suit your needs, press the knob. This will bring you back to the main face screen. From here, tap the face. Your new face should now appear with all its customizations. If you added options for calendar and weather, you can now tap those options to bring up more detailed views. To bring up the more detailed view, tap your finger on the icon on the screen (e.g., to see the weather, for instance, tap the weather icon).

And remember, anytime you want to know the time anywhere else in the world, just lift your wrist and say, "what time is it in…?"

## Watch Faces and What They Do

Every face has different details that can be added or removed. Below is a list of the current watch faces and what you can add to them. Watch face that have status icons can be touched to load the associated app.

You may notice that many of the faces below don't show up when you firm press to change the watch face. That's because only the most commonly ones appear. Swiping all the way over brings up New; tap that, and then use the digital crown to scroll through all the other faces.

### Activity Digital

This is the face to use when working out. It measures your progress but has an overlay of a clock to give you the time as well.

## Breathe

Unleash the yogi in you; this simplistic watch face has one goal: encourage you to breathe.

## Mickey Mouse

Featuring Mickey Mouse (now with Minnie Mouse), this is certainly the most whimsical and animated watch experience. Tap him and he will speak the time--if sound is on. The following can be added to the face: date, calendar, moon phase, sunrise / sunset, weather, activity summary, alarm, timer, stopwatch, battery charge, world clock, stocks.

**Toy story**

Not to be outdone by the Mickey app, is the Toy Story app. Tap the screen to get a different whimsical animation.

**Modular**

A very modern-looking face with lots of room to add things. The following can be adjusted: color. The following features can be added: calendar, moon phase, sunrise /sunset, weather, stocks, activity summary, alarm, timer, stopwatch, battery charge, world clock.

**Motion**

This is one of the few Apple Watch faces that is fully animated. You can pick between a butterfly, flower, and jellyfish. The following can be added to the face: date.

### Simple

As the name implies, this is the simplest classic watch face. The following can be adjusted on the face: color of the sweep hand and the numbering of the dial. The following can be added: date, calendar, moon phase, sunrise / sunset, weather, activity summary, alarm, timer, stopwatch, battery charge, and world clock.

### Solar

Bring out your inner scientist with this app, which displays the sun's position in the sky.

## Utility

A very basic and classic looking face; the following features can be changed: the color of the second hand and the numbering on the dial. The following can be added to the face: date, calendar, moon phase, sunrise / sunset, weather, activity summary, alarm, timer, stopwatch, batter charge, world clock, stock.

## X-Large

X-Large is the most simplistic modern face—it's also the boldest looking. The following can be adjusted: color.

## Chronograph

Measures the exact time in increments.

## Explorer

This face is a cellular exclusive. The goal of the watch face is to show you the cell signal strength.

## Fire and Water

Animates with smoke whenever you life it.

## Infograph

This is an Apple Watch Series 4 exclusive face; it gives you a wealth of info at your wrist--time in another city, UVI index, weather, etc.

## Kaleidoscope

The faces changes patterns based on your preference.

## Liquid Medal

Animates with a melting medal whenever you lift your wrist.

## Pride

Shows the colors of Pride.

## Astronomy

This watch face shows you the exact position for different planets and displays day, date and time.

## Chronograph

A very precise and classic watch face that includes a stopwatch that can be activated from the watch face. The following can be adjusted: dial details and face color. You can also add the following to the face: date, moon phase, sunrise / sunset, calendar, weather, stock, activity summary, alarm, timer, battery charge, world clock.

## Color

A very basic face whose primary feature is changing the colors. The following can be adjusted: Dial color. The following can be added to the face: date, moon phase, sunrise / sunset, weather, activity summary, stopwatch, timer, battery charge, world clock, your monogram.

## Photos

The best watch face for last in many people's opinions: photos. Photos let's you show a slideshow of photos and the time. So everytime you lift your wrist, something new awaits. Live photos even have animations!

To add this face, swipe all the way to the left of all the watches faces, and then tap New.

Now scroll down to Photo, and tap once.

If you want to show only one particular photo, then open the photo app on your watch.

Scroll to the photo you want. In the bottom corner of the photo below, you'll see an icon in the lower right corner a circle with dots—this indicates that the photo is a Live Photo and will be animated as an Apple Watch face.

Once it's on the screen, firm press. This will bring up an option to make it the watch face.

You can make it a normal watch face, or a abstract on (kaleidoscope).

If you want to remove a Watch Face, just go to change the face as you normally would and swipe up.

# [7]

# SHOW ME WHAT THIS WATCH IS CAPABLE OF...BUT KEEP IT RIDICULOUSLY SIMPLE

This chapter will cover:
- Sending / receiving messages
- Reading / sending email
- Using Siri
- Making phone calls
- Adding calendar events
- Setting reminders
- Using the map
- Using photos
- Listening to music
- Looking up the weather
- Setting alarms and timers
- Using the Apple Watch with the Apple TV

- Using the Apple Watch as a Walkie-Talkie

## Messages

The first thing you should know about Messages is this isn't the place to type an epic love note. It's the place where you send quick replies. Technically you could do something a little grander, but the time and effort involved makes it rather fruitless.

To begin a new message, go to your watch's home screen by pressing the knob, tap the Message icon, and press and hold your finger firmly on the screen. After three seconds it will ask if you'd like to start a new message.

From here, tap the "Add a contact". Once you pick your contact, tap "Create message."

There's a few ways you can create a message. The first is dictate it. When you dictate it, it's listen to what you say and transcribes it--not always accurately (especially if it's noisy)

The second way is to scribble it. When you scribble it, you write the letter one at a time. If you need to change a letter, you can delete it, or tap it and scroll through more choices.

Next is the reply with taps. This is good if you are trying to get the attention of someone else who is also wearing an Apple Watch. They feel whatever tap vibration you send them.

Finally, you can reply with an emoji.

Underneath the four ways to reply is common phrases to reply with. Tap an of them and it will add it to the message.

When you receive a message, Apple Watch will tap you. Move your hand toward you and the message will appear automatically; once you put your hand down, it turns off again. Use the watch's side knob to scroll through the message. You'll have the same methods to reply that you did when I showed how to write a message (above).

The biggest difference is Apple Pay is an option now. Apple Pay lets you send money to someone. So if you are out to lunch with a friend, you can pay your share of the bill right from the watch.

If no reply is needed, then hit the Dismiss button instead of the Reply button.

If you are not getting messages on your watch, then chances are a Setting is not enabled; you can change the Message setting from the Apple Watch app on your iPhone.

## Reading and Sending Email

When you get mail, you'll also get a notification; but there's also an app for reading and managing your email. As it is on the iPhone, the email app is simply named "Mail."

To start, go to the app on your home screen and tap on it. It looks pretty bare bones, but there's a lot to it. You can scroll through your messages from within the app. To read a message, tap it.

At any time, you can continue reading the message on your iPhone, by swiping up on the Mail icon in the lower left corner of your iPhone's lock screen (Note: handoff does need to be set up, so refer to how to set up handoff in this book if you haven't already).

While Apple Watch does support HTML formats (including different fonts and font colors), it still might look a little off, so for a complex message, the iPhone is the best place to read them.

If it's a long message, you can use the Digital Crown knob to scroll through it.

When a message includes phone numbers or address, the watch will automatically recognize it and turn it into a hyperlink. Tapping on them will either bring up the Phone or Map app (depending on what the hyperlink is).

To reply to a message, you will need to use the iPhone to compose it.

## Managing Mail

### Flag an Email

When you are reading an email on the watch, you can press firmly on the display, and then tap Flag. You can also flag a message from your message list by swiping the message to the left, then tapping on More.

### Mark as Unread

If you want to mark a message as unread, go to your message list, swipe left, tap More, and then tap Unread.

### Delete an Email

If you want to delete a message, go to your message list, swipe left, tap More, and then tap Trash. (Note: if your email is set up to archive a message, then you'll see the Archive button instead of the Trash button.)

### Selecting the Inboxes that Appear

You may not want all of your mail to appear on your phone. Let's say you have a work email, family email, and spam email, and you only want your family email to appear. If that's the case then go to the Apple Watch app on your iPhone, tap My Watch, and then go to Mail and Include Mail. Specify which mailbox you do or do not want to appear.

### Customize Alerts

If you want to change how you are alerted when you get mail (or if you don't want alerts at all), then go to the Apple Watch app on your iPhone, and tap My Watch, then turn on Mail Alerts and Show Alerts. Sound would be alerts that make noises and Haptic is alerts that vibrate.

### Message List

If you find your email message list is simply too long, you can reduce the number of lines of the preview by going to the Apple Watch app, tapping on My Watch and then going to Mail and Message Preview; pick 2 lines of message, 1 line of message or no lines of a message.

## Siri

If you love Siri on the iPhone, you're going to love her even more on your wrist. Don't love her? Give her a second chance because she got a little bit of an upgrade.

You can access Siri one of two ways (you'll quickly discover that there are multiple ways to do most tasks on the watch):

1.  Press the Digital Crown knob.
2.  Raise your wrist and speak (say good-bye to "Hey Siri") then say your request (e.g. "what's the weather in Paris?" "Who won last night's Yankee game?"); you can use Siri to open apps, set alarms, call friends—pretty much anything you can think of. With no on-board keyboard, Siri is more important than ever.

## Making Phone Calls

While you may not go out and buy and Apple Watch to get your Dick Tracy on and make phone calls from your wrist, it's certainly a nice touch...and it's pretty simple to do.

Once your watch is in sync with your iPhone, you are ready to start making and receiving calls.

If a call comes in, you can mute it by placing your hand over the watch. If you want to send it to your phone or reply with a text, then move your finger over the digital crown and scroll to the bottom.

To answer the call, use the green button; to decline the call, press the red one. It's just like getting a call on your iPhone. Your watch will use a built in microphone when you speak into it. It's not the best quality, but it gets the job done.

To make a call, you have three options:

Go to your home screen and tap the phone icon.

The other option is the easiest; that option is to use Siri. Just lift your wrist and say, "call PERSON'S NAME." If the wrong person is dialed, just hit the Hang Up button and if you do it quickly enough, the call won't go through.

## Calendar

The Calendar app calendar icon on Apple Watch shows events you've scheduled or been invited to today and for the next week. Apple Watch shows events for all calendars you use on your iPhone.

To view your calendar, open the Calendar app on your home screen; you can, also swipe up from your watch face to bring up Glances, and swipe until you get to the Calendar glance. You can also tap on the day's date on the watch face if you've added that option.

You can also see what's going on in your day by lifting your wrist and saying, "Siri tell me what's going on today.

To switch between the daily events and single list of events, press firmly on the display while you are in the Calendar app, then tap List or Day.

To view a different day, just go to Day view while in the Calendar app, and then swipe left to see the next day's events.

If you want to see the full month, then tap on the < in the upper left corner of the Calendar app, and then tap the monthly calendar; repeat the step to go back to Day view. When you are in Month view, any days that you have an activity will be highlighted in red.

### Adding Events
To add an event, you will need to open the Calendar app on your iPhone. If you are in the Calendar app on your watch, then a Calendar icon will appear on your iPhone's lock screen—just swipe up and it will go immediately to your Calendar.

You can have Siri add an event for you.

## Responding to Event Invites

When you get an invite to an event, it will appear as a notification; just swipe it or turn the Digital Crown knob when you see it, and then tap Accept, Maybe, or Decline.

The invite will also have the event organizer; to email the event organize, press firmly on the display while you are looking at the event details; you will be able to either send them a voice message or call them.

To adjust any of your Calendar's settings, go to the Apple Watch app on the iPhone, then tap My Watch, and finally tap Calendar.

## Reminders

If you use reminders on the iPhone, then you might be disappointed to see there is no Reminders app on the Apple Watch.

Reminders, however, is sort of there; while no app exists, if you create a reminder on your iPhone through the Reminders App, it will also remind you on your watch.

You can also create a reminder on your watch by using Siri; just lift your wrist and say "Hey Siri, set a reminder."

## Map

There are a couple of ways to use the map on your Apple Watch; the first and quickest is to swipe up from your watch face to bring up Glances and then swipe to the Map Glance. From here you'll see your current location and what's around you; you can use the Digital Touch knob to zoom in or out. To scroll/pan through the map, use your finger. If you tap the arrow in the bottom left corner, the current location will be updated.

To search the map, tap and hold your finger over the map; this will let you speak what you want to find or see your most recent locations.

You can tap any location that appears on your map to get directions to it or more information about it. You can also stick a pin in an area that you want to go. To add a pin, just touch and hold Map (not firmly) and wait for the pin to drop. If you tap the pin after it's been dropped, it will give you the address. To move the pin, just hover over a new location and drop a new pin. If you aren't sure what someone's address is, if you drop a pin near their address, you can get an approximate address.

### Directions

Turn by turn directions on the Apple Watch is one of the bigger features, and it's really simple to use.

When you get a text with an address, the address is automatically converted to a hyperlink;

click on it, and a map will immediately open. You can zoom in and out of the map by turning the Digital Crown knob.

If you don't have a message with the address, then go to your watch's Home screen, tap the Maps icon; the map will appear showing your current location. To find an address, tap your finger firmly on the screen. You'll get an option to either search for the address or use one of your contacts' addresses. When you search for an address, it will give you the option to use a recently used address, or speak the address through dictation.

When the address comes up, there will be two options: driving directions and walking directions. Walking will not only change the time it will take, but also take you down paths a car cannot go. Once you make your selection by tapping, just hit the Start button.

One of the cool features about the map is the turn-by-turn direction. When it's time to make a turn, your watch will tap you to get your attention. Even more cool is if you start directions on your phone, it will also appear on your watch.

**Photos**

To view photos on the Apple Watch, go to the Photos app on your watch home screen; because the watch cannot actually take photos, the photos you see will be the ones from your iPhone album.

By default, the watch is set to display only your Favorites album, but you can change this.

Once the app is open, just tap the photo you want to view and use the Digital Crown knob to zoom in or out, and use your finger to pan it. Zoom all the way out to see all of your photos.

### Pick an Album

If you'd like to choose another album to show on your watch then open the Apple Watch app on the iPhone and tap My Watch, then go to Photos and Synced Album; pick the album you want to sync; you can also create a new album using photos from your phone.

### Storage

The watch does not have as much space as your phone so it's important to limit how much you store on it; to limit photo storage, open the Apple Watch app on the iPhone, tap My Watch, then go to Photos and Photo Limits.

You can see how many photos are currently on your Apple Watch by opening the Settings app from the watch's main screen, tapping General, and then About. You can also see this on your phone by opening the Apple Watch app, then tapping My Watch, General, and About.

## Camera Viewfinder

While the watch doesn't have a camera built in, it does have a pretty awesome feature that lets you use the watch as an external camera viewfinder and shutter to your iPhone camera.

For this to work, you need to make sure the watch is no more than 30 ft. from your iPhone.

To take a photo, open the Camera app on your watches home screen, then position the iPhone to frame the shot using the Apple Watch as your viewfinder. If you want to change the exposure, just tap the area you want to focus on from your Apple Watch preview; tap the shutter button on your watch. You can preview the photo on your watch, but the photo will actually be saved on the iPhone.

Next to the shutter button is a timer button; if you want to do a timed shot, tap that; the timer takes burst shots, which is great for action / sports photos.

## Music

The music app is, of course, on your home screen, but you can reach it more quickly by swiping up on your screen.

Like almost anything on the Watch, you can also play music with Siri. Just lift your wrist and say, "play Bob Dylan."

When music is playing, tap the top corner and you'll have the option to scroll through Artist, Albums, Playlist and Songs (scroll using the Digital Crown knob).

The watch automatically syncs to your phone and will play music that's on your iPhone. That's great when your phone is nearby, but sometimes you don't have your phone nearby and want to listen to music directly on your watch. You can load music to your Watch pretty easily.

To add music, connect your watch to its charger, then open the Apple Watch app on your iPhone. Next, tap Music (it's near the bottom). After that, tap "sync playlist," and choose the songs you want to add.

To play music directly from your watch, open the music app and press firmly on the screen when the app opens. This will open a new menu with four options: Shuffle, Repeat, Source, and Airplay. Select "Source." Next select Apple Watch. It will now walk you through pairing your watch with Bluetooth headsets to listen to the music.

From the previous menu, you can also select Airplay to pair your watch with an Airplay enabled speaker.

## Stocks

If you'd like to monitor one or more stocks from your watch, open the Stock app; you can see details about a stock by tapping it in a list and then turning the Digital Crown to scroll.

You can also use Siri to find a stock price by saying "what was the closing price for XYZ stock?"

You can also see stock as a glance by swiping up from your watch face, and swiping to the Stock glance. From here you can also add stock.

## Weather

There are a couple of ways to check weather on your watch; one of the easiest is to swipe up from your watch face to bring up Glances, and then find the Weather Glance.

If you want more detailed weather information, then go to the Weather app by opening it on the watch home screen. The Weather app will have 10-day forecast, current temperature and conditions, and chance of rain.

The Weather app is synced to your iPhone, so if you want to add or remove a city, then do it from your phone.

You can change the default city being shown on your watch by opening the Apple Watch app on your iPhone, tapping on My Watch, and then going to Weather and Default City.

## Activity

One of the features that Apple is really promoting with the Apple Watch is Activity; one of the reasons to wear the watch, if you are to believe Apple, is to get you to move more. It's a hard sell with me, because I'm a lazy bum!

The app is divided up into three fitness goals: stand up for at least one minute of every hour, hit your calorie burn goal by moving more (you can set your goal), and accumulate 30 minutes of an activity that requires movement above a brisk walk. Each of these goals makeup rings; as you complete these goals, the rings begin to fill up, and by the end of the day they should ideally be full.

To get started, go to your home screen and tap the Activity app. The first time that you open the app, it will give you a very short tutorial on what the app is and how it helps you live a happier, healthier life. Once you finish the tutorial, you'll have to enter some personal information—this is for your eyes only and you only do it once. It will help ensure the app is as accurate as possible. For each section, turn the Digital Crown to enter your information.

After you've finished, you will indicate your activity level; you can change this later, so if you aren't sure, then go for lower—not higher. Next you'll see your suggested goal, which you can accept or adjust. When you are done, tap Start Moving. Your app will now be tracking you in the background. There's no need to start anything each day.

You can access the Activity app at any time by tapping on it from your home screen. The first thing you'll see is all the rings together. You can use your digital crown to see more detail information on the rings.

At any time, you can change your goals by opening the app, then pressing firmly on the display. You can also have reminders sent to you to encourage you to complete your goal.

In the Activity app on your iPhone, you can view your Activity history, and see more detailed reports about what you've done. The measurements will get more accurate as you wear the watch more, and it gets to know your behaviors.

Finally, if you swipe left on the activity app, you can share your activity goals; perfect for the lazy bum like me, who likes to remind his spouse that they were sitting around all day.


## Workout

Workout is kind of a companion to Activity even though there's a separate app for it. The point of it is to help you track progress during a workout session and help you hit new milestones.

From your Home screen, tap the Workout app and you'll immediately see dozens of different workouts. They range from brisk walks to more intense workouts—both indoor and outdoor. For indoor and outdoor running or walking and outdoor cycling, you can also set a distance goal. You can also choose no goal and simply get started.

The following are the workouts you can choose from:

- Outdoor walk
- Outdoor run
- Outdoor cycle
- Indoor walk
- Indoor run
- Indoor cycle
- Elliptical
- Rower
- Stair stepper
- High intensity interval training
- Hiking

- Yoga
- Pool swim
- Open water swim
- Other (no, this isn't where you track the fitness goal "watch TV")

You can either start the workout or set goals. To set a goal (such as how far you want to walk), tap the three dots.

This will bring up four options: open, calories, distance, time.

What these options will do is set a goal. So, as an example, let's say my goal is to walk three miles; I add three miles, then tap begin, and it will start tracking. I'll get alerted when I hit three miles.

Once you hit Begin, the watch will immediately count down to the start. During your workout, a ring will steadily fill in here as you approach your goal.

To pause or end the workout, just press firmly on the display and press End or Pause. When you end the workout, you can scroll through a full summary. You can either save the data or discard it.

Check Your Heart Rate

To get the best results with your heart rate, make sure the watch is tight enough to touch the skin, but not too tight.

It will measure your heart rate when you load the app.

Taping on any of the three options: current, resting rate, or walking average will get you an overview of your heart rate.

If you are in a workout, you can check your heart rate by swiping on the lower half of the Workout progress screen.

## Set Alarms

If you want to set an alarm, go to the Alarm Clock app from your watch's home screen.

Once it's open, press firmly on the display, then tap New +. Tap Change Time (remember to also change AM / PM); you can use the Digital Crown knob to adjust the hours and minutes. Finally tap Set. You can tap the < in the upper left corner to return to the alarm settings, where you can repeat an alarm, push snooze, or label it.

To adjust an alarm, tap the Alarm Clock app, then tap the alarm in the list that you want to change. Tap next to the alarm to turn it on or off. You can delete an alarm by tapping on then alarm, then scrolling to the bottom and tapping Delete.

## Use a Timer

To use the watch's timer, go to the home screen and tap Timer; timers can be set for up to 24 hours. To set a timer, open the app, tap hours or minutes, turn the Digital Crown knob to adjust the time, and finally tap Start. If the timer will be more than 12 hours, then while adjusting the timer press firmly on the display and tap 0-24 hours.

## Use the Stopwatch

If you want to use the stopwatch to time things like the time of a track lap, then go to your home screen and tap Stopwatch app. To start the watch, tap the Start button; tap the lap button to split the time or record a lap. Timing will continue as you switch between them. When you are finished, tap Reset.

You can also pick the format for the stopwatch; there are four different ones: Analog, Digital, Graph, and Hybrid.


## Remote Control

A lesser-known fact about the watch is that it doubles as a remote control iTunes and Apple TV.

Before you begin make sure both your watch and your device are using the same network; if your phone is using one Wi-Fi and your watch is using another, then they won't work.

### Remote Play iTunes

If you'd like to use the watch as a remote for iTunes on your Mac, open up the Remote app; next tap the Add Device+.

In iTunes on your computer, click the Remote button near the top of the iTunes window; it will ask you to enter the 4-digit code that is now displayed on your watch. (Note: if you look for the Remote button in iTunes before you tap Add Device on the Apple Watch, you'll be waiting a long time—it will only appear after you tap Add Device; also make sure iTunes is up-to-date.)

### Remote for Apple TV

If you'd like to use the watch as a remote for iTunes on your Apple TV, open up the Remote app; next tap the Add Device+. (Note: remember you must be using the same Wi-Fi Network.)

On your Apple TV go to Settings, and then General, and finally Remote, and select the Apple Watch; enter the passcode that's currently on your watch.

## Walkie-Talkie

WatchOS 5 makes it a whole lot easier to communicate with those close with it's Walkie-Talkie feature. To use it, both people need to have an Apple Watch Series 1 or later and watchOS 5. You also need to turn on FaceTime because you will be using FaceTime Audio.

Unfortunately, this feature is not available in all countries.

The first time you use the app, you will need to add friends. Open the app. Tap , then choose a contact.

Now wait. It's not like a phone call where it connects right away with your friend. They have to give permission to you to reach them. It will stay gray until the person accepts. Once they accept you can start talking away instantly.

To remove a friend, open the Walkie-Talkie app, swipe left on the friend, then tap ✖. Or open the Apple Watch app on your iPhone, tap Walkie-Talkie > Edit, tap ⊖, then tap Remove.

To start a conversation, just open the app, tap the friends name (after they've accepted, and wait for it to connect (they have to be wearing the watch). Once connected, tap the talk and say something, then let go when you are done.

You can turn the volume up and down with the Digital Crown.

If you no longer want to talk over this feature, just open it and toggle it to off; if a contact tries to reach you, it will say you are unavailable.

If you turn on Silent Mode, you can still hear the person's voice and the chimes that come in. If you turn on Theater Mode or Do Not Disturb then it will make you unavaliable to talk.

# [8]

# WHAT OTHER THINGS SHOULD I KNOW ABOUT THE APPLE WATCH?

This chapter will cover:
- Accessibility features
- How to care for the Apple Watch
- How to reset the Apple Watch
- How to update the Apple Watch

Like every Apple product, the Apple Watch has accessibility features to help people with disabilities.

It works very similar to your iPhone; to access the features, go to the Apple Watch app on your iPhone, then My Watch, then General, and finally Accessibility.

**VoiceOver**

VoiceOver helps you use the watch even if you can't see the watch. It will read back everything that's on the watch for you. You can turn it on by going to the Settings app on the watch's home screen, then General, Accessibility, and finally VoiceOver.

When VoiceOver is on, you can move your finger around the display and listen to the name of each item you touched. VoiceOver also uses different gestures; you can go back by using two fingers to draw a "Z" shape on the display. To open an app, you will double tap it instead of single tap. To pause the VoiceOver from reading what's on the screen, tap the display with two fingers; tap with two fingers again to resume play.

When you set up your watch for the first time, you can use VoiceOver as well. When you turn on the watch for the first time, press the side button; after it turns on, triple click the Digital Crown knob.

**Zoom**

The watch is a small display—perhaps even smaller than you thought it would be—so it's understandable that you might want the display a little bigger. If that's the case, go to the Settings app, and then turn on General, Accessibility, and Zoom.

To zoom in or out when Zoom is enabled you will double-tap the display with two fingers. To move around (or pan) the display, you will drag with two fingers.

## Bold Text

Putting the text in boldface is another way to make reading the text on your screen a little easier. You can make the text boldface by going to the Settings app on your home screen, then tapping General and Accessibility and turning on Bold Text; the watch will need to be restarted before this goes into effect.

## Handling

### Removing the Bands

To change a band, press the band release button on the Apple Watch, and slide the band across, then slide in the new band. You should never force a band into the slot, as this could get it stuck.

It is recommended that you fit the band so it is close to your skin, but not so tight that it is squeezing your wrist.

**Band Care**

Apple recommends that you clean the leather portions of bands with a nonabrasive, lint-free cloth that is, if necessary, dampened with water. The band should not be attached to the watch. After cleaning, let the band dry before reattaching to the watch. Do not store leather in direct sunlight or in high temperatures or high humidity; you also should not soak the leather in water as it is not water resistant.

For all other bands, Apple recommends cleaning the same way, but the band should be dried with a nonabrasive, lint-free cloth.

## A Little More Advanced

**Force Restarting the Apple Watch**

In very rare cases, the Apple Watch may freeze or need to be force restarted. If this ever happens, hold down the side button and Digital Crown knob at the same time for ten seconds. When the Apple Logo appears, you can let go.

**Resetting the Watch Settings**

If you want to reset the watch settings and make the watch new (remember this erases everything) then go to the Settings app from the Home screen, then go to General, Reset, and finally Erase All Content and Settings. Once it's reset you will need to pair it with your phone again. Make sure you do this if you ever sell or give your watch or phone away, as your vital information (like credit cards) will be available to that person if you don't.

### Get Your Watch DNA

If you need to know what model number your watch is, what software version it is, what its serial number is, or what its capacity is then go to the Settings app from your Home screen, and then General and About.

### Update Apple Watch Software

Much like the iPhone and iPad, updates to the Apple Watch software are done over the air— meaning you won't need to plug anything in.

To see if there's an update, open the Apple Watch app on the iPhone, then tap My Watch, General, and finally Software Updates. It will tell you if there's an update, and then you just follow the steps. Updates don't happen very often—usually just a handful of times each year.

# [9]

# SO MANY BANDS AND ACCESSORIES, SO LITTLE TIME

This chapter will cover:
- Official Apple Watch bands and accessories
- Unofficial Apple Watch bands and accessories

### Watch Bands & Accessories

What's a watch without its band? Unlike traditional bands, the Apple Watch makes it remarkably easy to switch out bands. And unlike any other Apple product, you have lots of options; normally an Apple product comes in two or three colors; with the watches there are several dozen ways to mix and match.

Below is a guide to all the different ones you have to choose from. (Note: when purchasing a band, remember that a 42mm band won't be compatible with a 38mm band or vice versa). Unless otherwise noted, all bands are available in both 38 and 42mm. Some bands are not one size fits all.

## Official Bands & Accessories

### Sport Band

It's available in black, space gray, white, pink, blue, green. The band is obviously best for working out; it's also the cheapest band available. It's made of fluoroelastomer, a synthetic rubber known for performing well in heat. Because this band isn't one size fits all, the chart below helps you make the right choice:

S/M  Fits wrists 130-180mm

M/L  Fits wrists 150-200mm

S/M  Fits wrists 140-185mm

M/L  Fits wrists 160-210mm

## Classic Buckle

This band is made of "Dutch leather" from a tannery in the Netherlands. Apple promises the mill gives it a distinctive texture. The closer is made of stainless steel.

## Milanese Loop

Apple says the inspiration for this stainless steel mesh band was a mesh band from 19th century Milan. The band is completely magnetic and easy to put on.

### Modern Buckle
Three sizes: small, medium, and large

It's available in brown, black, pink, and midnight blue. The leather for this stunning band comes from a French tannery established in 1803. How are the modern and classic bands different? The leather is slightly different, but the most noticeable difference is the buckle. The classic is a strap with holes; the modern is a magnetic band that helps you have a more precise fit. Because this band isn't one size fits all, the chart below helps you make the right choice:

**Link Bracelet**

One of the most expensive and complex band, this stainless steel band has over 100 parts. Apple claims the craftsmanship is so complex that it takes nine hours to assemble a single case. The magnetic closure is one size fits all.

**Leather Loop**
Only available for the 42mm band.

It's available in stone, light brown, bright blue, and black. Made of Venezia leather and hand-crafted in Arzignano, Italy, this band has a soft and gilded feel. The magnetic loop is easy to put on. Because this band isn't one size fits all, the chart below helps you make the right choice:

M  Fits wrists 150-185mm

L  Fits wrists 180-210mm

**Apple Watch Magnetic Charging Cable**
($29 for 1m cable; $39 for 2m cable)

Apple has only announced one official accessory for the Apple Watch, and that is an extra charger (one comes free with your watch).

## Unofficial Bands

There's no denying the Apple Watch bands are slick…but they're also expensive. If you want to complement your watch with something a little less pricey, lots of options have already popped up, and many more are coming.

### Casetify

Click has a collection of bands for $50. For the same price, you can also customize your band and add your own photos for a truly unique fashion statement.

### Click

Click is a $10 component that attaches to your Apple Watch and lets you and any band you want-- so if you have a nice traditional band in your closet, this is a great option for you.

### Monowear Design

Monowear Design promises to have Apple style for not Apple prices. A leather or linked band that looks surprisingly similar to Apple's bands can be purchased for less than $100.

## Reserve Strap

If you are worried about battery usage on the Apple Watch, then Reserve Watch might be for you. The $249.99 promises to give your watch more juice (no mention of how much at this writing). This watch is currently available for pre-order, but it's not yet known when the band will be released.

## Pod by Nomad

For people wanting to charge their watch on the go without the $249 band strap price tag, there's also the Pod by Nomad, which is priced at $59.95. This small device can easily fit in purse or briefcases, and promises to charge your watch four times before needing a recharge itself.

### X-doria

There are already several bumper guards for the Apple Watch (which help shield your watch from scratches much like a case). One is the $29.99 Defense Edge.

### Var Cyclip

The Var Cyclip promises to be perhaps the first accessory that lets you attach your watch to a handlebar (whether bike, moped, or motorcycle). No word at this writing about the price or availability.

### Calypso Timeless

You paid a lot for your watch, so why not show it off? If you want a classy stand for your watch, check out the Calypso Timeless -- a $129 stand.

These are some of the many bands available, but look for hundreds of other options as months go by.

# [10]

# APPLE CARES?

This chapter will cover:
- What's covered under the standard Apple Watch warranty
- What's Apple Care?

## Warranty

Because of how delicate the watch can be it's important to understand what's covered and what's not covered under the watch warranty.

### Covered

Debris under the display glass or pixel anomaly; the back cover is removed but there is no damage (by damage, there should be absolutely no evidence that the cover was removed by prying); and finally, condensation in the heart rate sensor windows.

### Covered With Fees
Damages that are covered out-of-warranty include cracked, missing, removed, or damaged Digital Crown cap; abrasions, puncture holes, missing buttons from a drop, chips in the display, a removed back cover with damage, a bent band enclosure, a missing band release, or any cracks on the back cover.

Fees do apply to these services, and the cost depend on the model and if you have AppleCare +.

### Ineligible for Service
The following damages are considered ineligible for warranty services: disassembling unit or missing parts, catastrophic damage, counterfeit or third-part parts, and lastly unauthorized modifications. (Note: catastrophic damage may be covered with AppleCare+; check with the Apple Store and explain the situation; it's provided at their discretion).

## AppleCare
Every Apple Watch does come with AppleCare; for extended service, however, AppleCare also offers AppleCare+.

What's the difference? The free level care includes a one year limited warranty for hardware repairs and 90 days of free technical support. AppleCare+ extends the warranty for two years. For the pricier Apple Watch Edition, this warranty is extended an additional year. With AppleCare+ you get two incidences of accidental damage (fees do apply).

Before paying for AppleCare, one thing you should consider doing is checking the services your credit card offers; some credit cards will offer warranty extensions if you use their card for purchase. Some even consider loss or theft (which, by the way, AppleCare+ does not cover).

So is AppleCare+ worth it? Personally, I like it for peace of mind; I don't have to worry about expensive cases or banging the watch on something. Apple Stores have terrific customer support when it comes to AppleCare+.

As companies learn about what makes the watch tick, then services are bound to pop up that offer repairs more cheaply than what AppleCare charges, but Apple will always be the simplest way to repair your watch.

# APPENDIX: THE APPS

## Apple Apps

This book has covered all the important apps already on the phone, but for a quick overview, here they are again.

- Messages - This is where you will send and receive text messages (and also send and receive animated emojis).
- Phone - This is, obviously, where you make and receive calls, but it should be noted that when you are using the phone on your wrist, you can also transfer that call to your iPhone, so if you step into a place where speakerphone is frowned upon, you don't have to hang up and call back.
- Mail - You can read your mail message, but it's not for replying--it's more for managing mail (i.e., deleting, reading, flagging, and moving).

- Calendar - this app lets you quickly browse through your calendar and also accept and decline invitations.
- Activity -- this app is a bit of motivational workout app--it gives you a summary of how much you are standing, exercising, moving...in short it makes you feel guilty about how lazy you are.
- Workout -- when you are working out, you tell your watch what you are doing (running, walking, cycling) and then it shows you how far you've gone, and how fast you are going.
- Maps -- a turn-by-turn map...with a twist-- when it's time for you to turn, it taps you on the wrist.
- Passbook - This is essentially a micro version of Passbook for the iPhone, but instead of holding your phone to the scanner, you hold your wrist.
- Siri - Siri is one of the most important apps on the Apple Watch because with no keyboard, you need it to find things quickly; to use it, just lift your wrist and say "Hey Siri"-- no buttons need to be pressed to bring up Siri.
- Music- The music app is what you'd expect...unless you expect to plug in headsets; there's no audio input on the watch so you have to use Bluetooth headphones to listen.
- Camera Remote - The watch has no built in camera; what it has in its place is a

viewfinder, so if you want to take a selfie with your phone then you can use the watch to take the photo.

- Remote - If you have an Apple TV, this app lets you control it from your wrist; you can also use it to control your Mac or PC's iTunes library.
- Weather - Lets you see a visual summary of weather where you are or anywhere else in the world.
- Stocks - With this app you can see stock performance for up to six months.
- Photos - This is where you will view all your favorite photos.
- Alarm / Stopwatch / Timer - These are three relatively simple apps that do exactly what you'd expect them to do.
- World Clock - while the watch's time face screen is the main feature, it does have a second app for tracking time around the world.
- Settings - This is where you can turn off Wi-Fi, Bluetooth, etc.

## Non-Apple Apps

Chances are you've heard about all the popular apps for the Apple Watch already. I'm talking about Twitter, Instagram, etc. So below, I'm putting some of my favorite apps that you might not have heard of.

### SwipeSpeare

SwipeSpeare puts Shakespeare's words into modern English with a swipe; when you launch the app, you pick your play and then you are asked if you want to read it in modern English or the original language. Any time you want to see what the passage says in the other translation, you just swipe your finger across the passage. It includes a free copy of Romeo and Juliet too! The watch app syncs your notes, bookmarks, and highlights.

### SwipeBible

There aren't a lot of Bible apps for the watch yet. You probably know about all the popular ones, but one you might not have heard of is SwipeBible; it's from the makers of SwipeSpeare and it's entirely free. It lets you open up to nine Bible translations at the same time and toggle between the translations by swiping over the verse. The companion app is much like SwipeSpeare and lets you manage notes, bookmarks, and highlights.

### Do Button

Always forgetting to do things like turning off the lights? Try this app, which helps keep your life a little more organized.

## Dating

Your love life is now on your phone. Two popular dating apps (OkCupid and Match Dating App) have already figured out a way to put your dating life on your wrist. Looking for love? Try these apps!

## Games

Games are not ideal for Apple Watch; however, a few have already figured out how to do it. One is BoxPop, which is both challenging and addicting. Word games are also a great fit; one word game that has already figure out how to make a nice game for the wrist is Letter Zap.

## PowerPoint

Apple has, of course, promoted their own software's app: Keynote. Not as much attention has been given to PowerPoint; the Microsoft app lets you use your watch as a remote to your Power-Point slides on your iPhone.

## CALC

Calculator is more than a calculator app; it also lets you figure out how much to tip at a restaurant. It's easy to use and pretty powerful for a watch app. It's free to download and $1.99 for premium features. If all you want to do is tip, then another nice app is Cow Tipper.

### Tasty Recipes

Reading is not always easy on the watch; while I don't recommend reading a book on the watch, recipes are a perfect fit; this lets you leave your watch in another room while making all your favorite dishes by giving you a step-by-step guide right on your watch.

### 7 Minute Workout

Apple has you covered with a great workout app—but if you want to change it up a little, or just looking for something that gets you exercised a little…quicker—then try this app. As the name implies it gives you an intense workout in just seven minutes.

### Day One

Writing is not what the watch was made for—so a journal app (priced at $4.99) seems like an odd thing to make an app for; still, this app is surprisingly intuitive and easy to use. You can make quick notes about where you are or use the watch's Mic to include writing.

Made in the USA
Columbia, SC
29 December 2019